# New York Energy

# Rich Hebron

# New York Energy

## Rich Hebron

## Books by Rich Hebron

*Homeless but Human*
*Primary Ponderings*

## Nuance & Notes Series

*Chicago Clarity*
*Paris Beauty*
*New York Energy*
*Los Angeles Dreams*
*Miami Magic*
*Milwaukee Sensibility*
*Mexico City Merriness*
*London Happening*

## Written by Rich Hebron
## Illustrated by Kenneth Ferguson

*Milly Moves to the Farm*
*The Boy and the Rocketship*

## Rich Edition Classics

*The Great Gatsby*

Rich Hebron is an American author. He has lived half his life in Chicago and the other half on a farm in rural Wisconsin. He fuses these backgrounds together to draw inspiration and live a meaningful life in a world accelerated by the internet and digital technology. He hosts the Rich Conversations Podcast where he explores self-development and talks with friends in art and science fields.

Connect with Rich: @richhebron

*For those who want to live life with energy*

# Author's Note

My first near-death experience happened on the farm. An oil line blew on the tractor and became engulfed in flames. I jumped from it. My second near-death experience occurred four years afterwards. This time, three men pointed Uzi guns at my face, threatening to shoot me. Fortunately, it was just another reminder that life will end—all our lives. So how do we want ours to be?

After initially going fast, with the adrenaline from the encounter lasting months, I decided to stop. The difference between speed and velocity is that velocity is speed in a direction. Anyone can go fast—especially in circles. But it takes skill and something deeper to channel energy with purpose. Refining purpose requires restarting at the beginning. Be open and see what's happening. Pursue curiosity and, above all, patience.

My curiosity led me to hotel lobbies. I spent time visiting different ones in downtown Chicago and just sat, observed, and wrote notes, often sipping espresso or red wine. An appreciation for details developed. Gratitude followed. Every thing was there for a reason. Nothing was a coincidence. The creators of the spaces aimed to evoke particular emotions and feelings in people. They staged a vibe.

I learned that design affects our mind and influences our culture. The whole of something is the result of individual things. From a pencil to a house. From a shoe to our cities. From a light fixture to our lives. The story of our life is the result of every individual decision we make. The universe is the result of every individual atom.

Beauty is the result of those small, individual components. Love is understanding those small, individual components.

My passion and appreciation for detail expanded from hotel lobbies to virtually everything in life and in people. But something I especially had fun with was observing the designs on building facades. My favorites were those resembling nature. They possessed the character I aspire to be: dynamic, flexible, playful, and fruitful. Things that are alive are adaptable. Things that are dead are stiff, rigid, and brittle. Since human beings are part of nature, the same is true for people and their ideas and perspectives.

I encourage you to reflect on the follow questions:

- *Are current environments failing to design nuance?*
- *If design affects culture, what are the ramifications of prioritizing cheap and fast?*
- *Is a society that ignores patience a healthy one?*
- *If individuality is abandoned, is Love too?*

This is a series called *Nuance & Notes*.
This is a book of nuance of New York with notes from my mind and observations in the world.

New York is the world in a city. New York is the greatest city in the world. There's a contagious buzz in the air. Humans are free to pursue, reach, and even fail. The city and its people fear less than others. Those who live in New York want to be there. It shapes an attitude. It raises the collective energy and fortifies unity. The significance of this cannot be overstated. New York is the most walkable city in America. Every step is momentous and transports us to the past, present, and future. New York is a beacon. It shows what humanity can become. It gives us hope to imagine. If New York is all right, the world is all right.

Shot on iPhone 13 Mini

Shared value and purpose
make differences small

**Rich Hebron**

Let's not disregard the footsteps
of those who walked here first

More people
More energy

**Rich Hebron**

Walking resolves most problems

Be grateful for what each individual gives

**Rich Hebron**

We're free to be

Are we in a hurry?
Be sure we're not lost

Our dream is a precious gift
from the universe

Gratitude and patience
are the building blocks
of a fulfilling journey

**Rich Hebron**

The fearless pause and smell the flowers

The bold shine the light from within
to the world

**Rich Hebron**

We can be better by being together

An individual is strong
A community is stronger

What will we find
if we observe the world around us?

If we're looking down,
we're not looking up

Hold our dream tight

Different dreams become one dream

**Rich Hebron**

Flaws confirm it's real

Live our life
so the efforts of the past are not in vain

Celebrate that no limit exists
outside of our mind

It won't hurt to say hi
to the person next to us

Sharing eye contact and a smile
can make a day great

We can learn from any one,
so let's keep an open mind and heart

**Rich Hebron**

Remember that often
people's actions stem from pain

Appreciate shared experiences,
and we'll never feel alone

**Rich Hebron**

Friendship is more cost effective
than loneliness

Identify the source of pain
and address it

Friendships solve more problems
than prescriptions

Move our body like our future depends on it

Go out with friends and have fun

Every one is going through some thing
Breathe and smile

Find things to do
so we're not bored

Exceed expectations by
acting in the present

Nothing brings people together
like a rat scurrying
across the subway platform

We're not being held back
as much as we think

What're we willing to give comfort up for?

Crack a smile
Share a laugh
Have some fun

People remember the laughs they shared most

Go for a walk and see what happens

Nature can be a state of mind

We don't know what we don't know

**Rich Hebron**

Know what we need to know
know what we don't need to know

If we can appreciate a rainy day,
we've grown wise

**Rich Hebron**

Before we can realize our dreams,
we must believe we can

Don't lose that sparkle from our eye

**Rich Hebron**

Phones can't send energy

Geography is relevant
Geography is irrelevant

**Rich Hebron**

One must be ready
for Love

Help others see opportunity

We can't feel energy through a phone
only the energy of an image

Don't consolidate resources
if we're scared to employ them

Being ready to love
Find one accepting of love

Education is the ability to see opportunity

Give up very good
for the opportunity of great

Humans love stories

Find reasons to be where we want to be

Becoming great isn't linear

**Rich Hebron**

Shine bright to attract light

Share great stories with each other

**Rich Hebron**

Mind is divine
Body is human

Knowing each step is significant
life becomes grander

We'll find what we're looking for

The world is here and so are we

We're so happy, we're floating

If we build great habits for our self,
we'll see the beauty in others

**Rich Hebron**

Our body is a horse
Our soul is the rider

Eat like a stallion
Move as divine

Gratitude and patience
Start there first

If it works it works
Fuss less about the route

**Rich Hebron**

In a bake off,
taste each competitor before voting

If we don't try we won't know

**Rich Hebron**

If we have purpose,
a bed has little purpose

Do something difficult

**Rich Hebron**

Be grateful for our failures
It will make all taste sweeter

Lights inspire, so let our light shine

We're drawn to people who fear less

Know their music know them

**Rich Hebron**

See the snow sparkle

Don't let others bring us down
Instead, bring them up

Know how to live analog and digital

We can choose how to react

Friends are valuable in infinite ways

Be inspired to do better and be better

**Rich Hebron**

Be prepared
for that first domino to fall

Meeting with friends restores energy

What would we choose to do if we were free?

People reveal their selves in their choices

Rich Hebron

We're not in control
of others' perceptions of us

We can breathe in a crowd or in solitude

Imagine our business
if we keep out of others'

Gossip is reflective of boredom

**Rich Hebron**

Life is easier with purpose

Don't complain about problems
Solve problems

**Rich Hebron**

Freedom is physical
Freedom is mental

Resilience will take us farther
than a piece of paper

Learn from observation and experience

How do we spend our ideal morning?
How do we spend our ideal evening?

**Rich Hebron**

Be with friends who spark inspiration

Boredom can spur bad habits
Use boredom with wisdom

View participation as an honor
rather than a drag

What information are we missing?

Resilient people often emerge
as the best people

The miles are not equal
between a paved path
and one that is not

**Rich Hebron**

Be present enough to notice
a bird that graces our presence

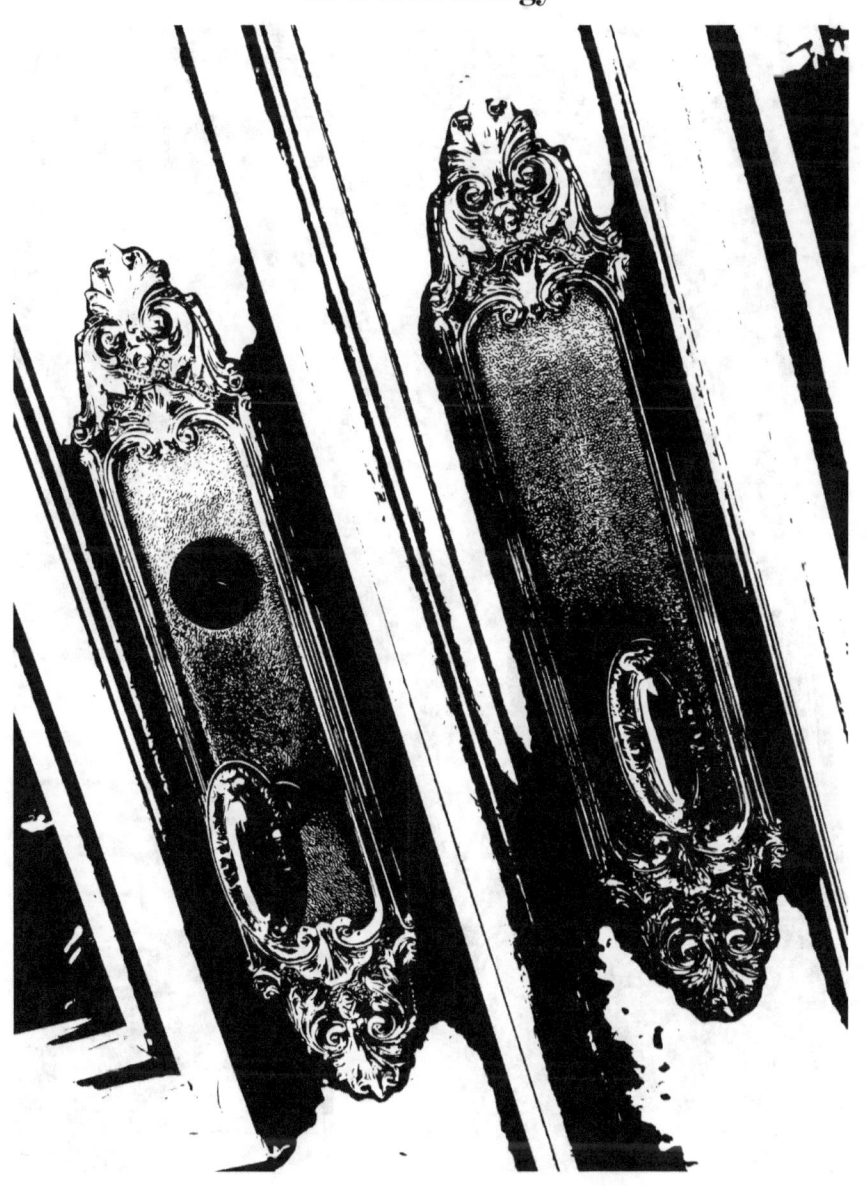

Think first before moving
Anyone can go fast in circles

Develop the mind
Develop skills
Develop our dreams

Give time to our self
to be useful to others

**Rich Hebron**

Who do we admire?
What qualities are consistent?

Have intention before looking at a screen

The artificial has no aroma

Live inside and outside of a bubble

The world would be so boring
if we were the same

The greatest singers surpass
our emotional threshold

# Rich Hebron

We're free to choose our future

Create time and space for pure focus

Purpose parts seas

Ordinary and extraordinary things
happen here

Purpose is not pursued
Purpose emerges
Purpose springs energy

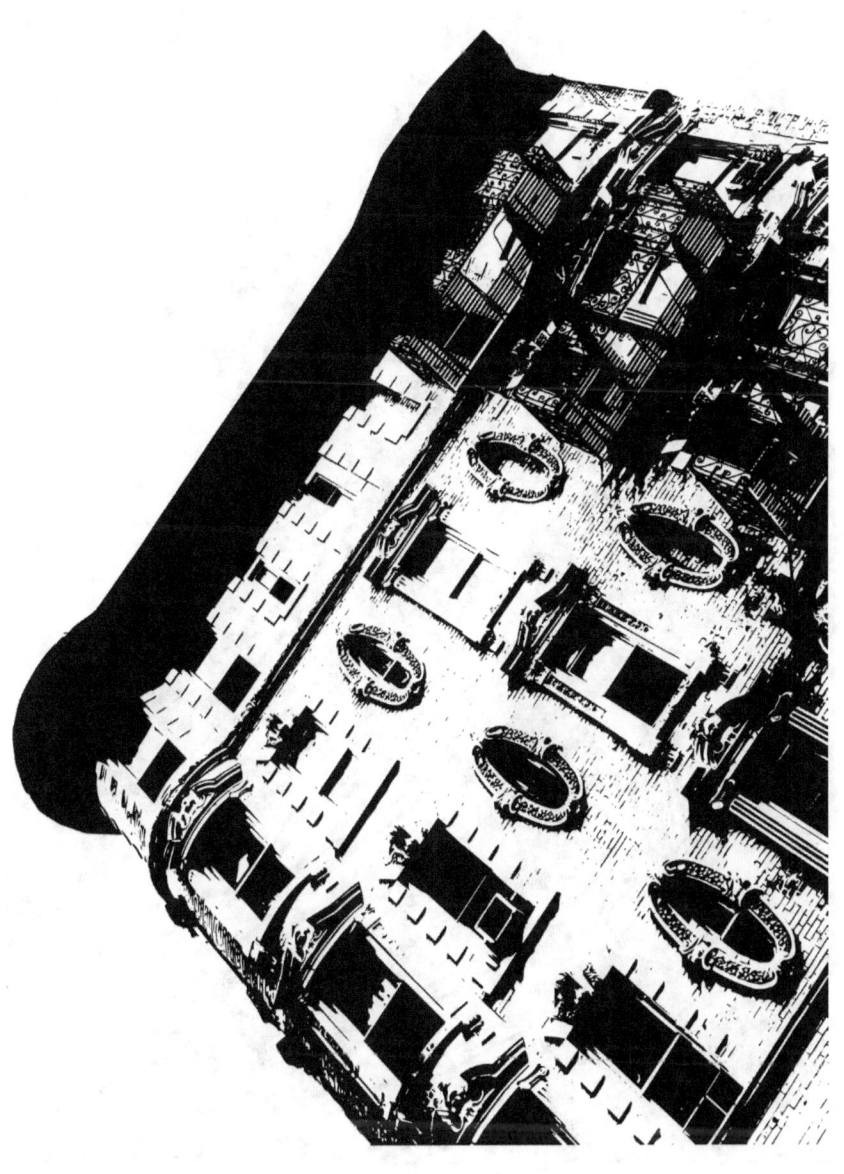

Begin with what we would regret

Potential is endless but the each day is not

Linear thinkers have ceilings

**Rich Hebron**

The thinking of something
is different than the doing something

Be calm and unmoved
See it happening

People crave feeling special
People long to belong

All our failures can
lead to one beautiful moment

Humility makes us significant

When a team is one,
there are no seams

# A Thought on Cities

Our cities are our greatest invention. They're the engines of civilization. Cities are the hubs that bring people, ideas, and opportunities together. They generate energy and inspire the pursuit of dreams and a better life.

I feel humans are meant to be isolated in nature or surrounded by other humans. Fusing the two maximizes energy and accelerates regenerative processes. This is why I shuffle between living on a farm in rural America and traveling to big international cities.

Having lived in Chicago for over 15 years, I am an enthusiastic advocate for urban living. I believe that the healthier the city, the more dynamic the society and culture. I'm passionate about exploring and analyzing the facets of each city. I believe in competition and that our cities should be constantly learning, adapting, evolving, and growing to serve and increase the quality of life for its residents. I love observing and comparing cities, noting their strengths and weaknesses, the effects of local geography, the movements and flows, and how every small matter contributes to the larger matter.

Cities are where big things happen. I believed this as a little kid growing up on a farm and I know it now as an adult who has experienced their impact.

I'm proud to combine notes that can help realize individual human potential with artwork that demonstrates the beauty collaboration can produce.

Rich leads weekly self-reflection sessions
to help people live with more energy

Join in on the Rich Conversations Podcast
or visit the Rich Hebron YouTube channel

Connect with Rich: @richhebron

# Notes

# Notes

# Notes

# Notes